M.R. Kruken

Safe and Meaningful use of Psychedelics

*A practical guide to beneficial psychedelic experiences*

# General introduction

In the evolving landscape of mental health and therapy, this small book aims to be a comprehensive but still down to earth and practical guide illuminating the path for individuals and therapists interested in exploring the therapeutic potential of psychedelics. With an increase in the acknowledgment of psychedelics for their profound impact on mental health treatment, renewed interest also emerges among the common man. This work aims to install basic guidelines for safe and informed practices for anyone venturing into these landscapes.

The book is divided into two primary sections. The first part delves into the basics, offering insights into the biochemistry of psychedelics, their historical context, and the subjective experience of a psychedelic trip. Hopefully the narrative brings forward the essence of psychedelics, challenging common misconceptions and highlighting their capacity to facilitate profound, life-altering experiences. The exploration of "set and setting," alongside the detailed accounts of the psychedelic experience, underscores the critical importance of preparation and environment in shaping these journeys.

In the second section, we make a transition to the pragmatic aspects of employing psychedelics in a therapeutic context – or one of general personal development. The focus is practical guidelines for conducting psychedelic sessions, emphasizing safety, preparation, and the pivotal role of the tripsitter. This section is particularly valuable for therapists and individuals alike, providing a structured approach to harnessing the therapeutic and developing potential of psychedelics while minimizing risks. The inclusion of topics such as the impact of music, the significance of altered states of consciousness, and strategies for integration, hopefully further enriches the reader's understanding and preparedness for psychedelic experiences.

# Part 1

# Introduction to psychedelics

*The only thing worse than being blind is having sight but no vision*
Helen Keller

The modern story behind psychedelics is by now summarized and repeated in countless books. Therefore, we will only briefly touch upon it here. The modern Western culture's acquaintance with these substances began in 1897 when the German chemist Arthur Heffter isolated and identified mescaline, a psychedelic substance found in the peyote cactus traditionally used by the indigenous people of what is now Mexico and parts of Texas. Ernst Späth synthesized the substance in 1919, and it wasn't until later in the 20th century that the substance's psychoactive effects began to attract attention in the West.

The British author Aldous Huxley played a significant role in popularization through his book "The Doors of Perception" from 1954, where he elaborates on his own experiences with mescaline. Thus, he introduced many in the West to the idea that the human mind could be explored with the help of psychedelic substances.Years earlier, the Swiss Albert Hofmann, a chemist working at the laboratories of the pharmaceutical company Sandoz, had synthesized lysergic acid diethylamide, better known as LSD. The substance was first synthesized in 1938 and then set aside, but quickly garnered renewed interest when Hofmann discovered its psychedelic effects in 1943 after accidentally absorbing microscopic amounts through his skin. Both scientific and military environments showed interest in the substance, and Hofmann himself would later call it his "problem child," understandably with good reason.

Hofmann also synthesized psilocybin in 1958, based on samples of mushrooms he received from the American mycologist Robert Gordon Wasson. Wasson had participated in mushroom ceremonies with members of Mexico's indigenous people, thus awakening to the substance's consciousness-expanding properties.

In the early 1960s, Timothy Leary and Richard Alpert, later known as Ram Dass, conducted experiments at Harvard University to study the effects of psilocybin in the Harvard Psilocybin Project. These studies, although controversial and resulting in Leary's dismissal, played a significant role in bringing psychedelics into the public eye. Also notable is Stanislav Grof, who has been a very important figure in systematizing the types of experiences people undergo under the influence of psychedelics and the implications this has for psychiatry and metaphysics. Grof has written numerous books, and much of the modern experimentation with both psilocybin and MDMA is based on his insights and protocols for safe and meaningful use of psychedelics.

Several ongoing studies were abruptly closed down as the United States put the "Controlled Substances Act" of 1970 into action, where LSD, psilocybin, and other psychedelics were categorized as "Schedule I substances," indicating high potential for abuse and no medicinal value. The ban applied not only to recreational use but also to research and treatment. From being part of a relatively promising field, those who still saw it as important and necessary to continue psychedelic research became criminals.

The so-called counterculture movement naturally played a significant role in provoking the ban. In the 1960s, psychedelics became an integrated part of the culture and lifestyle among many young people in the USA and Europe. They viewed these substances as tools for rebellion against the status quo, self-exploration, and spiritual enlightenment. During this time, psychedelics had a profound impact on the era's art and music, and countless creative individuals produced works reflecting the altered states of consciousness induced by these substances. Hardly any person can have avoided seeing or listening to these works. The impact history is far from insignificant, and it can even be argued that it has been a significant contribution to both the modern environmental movement, disarmament, and anti-nuclear weapons stance, general politics, and technological development. Neuroscientist David Nutt also points out how the first wave of psychedelics showed that chemical substances can indeed change human consciousness, paving the way for the modern psychopharmaceuticals that today are standard treatment for many mental disorders.

All this can at best only hint at what psychedelics are and how we should relate to them today. The culture and the norms are different today, and even though we today believe ourselves to be quite liberal, the truth is more complicated than that. For example, young people today are quite good friends with their parents and do not seem to be in the same kind of rebellion as in the 1960s – despite "climate roars" and other tentative attempts at countercurrent activities. At the same time, it is the case that young and adults generally have become very agreeable about what is true and false, right and wrong – in a way that may also entail a certain cultural stagnation.

Perhaps the age of social media's navel-gazing, easily offended, and anxiety-laden tendencies is also, in a way, an expression of this narrowing, although it is too simplistic to draw clear lines between cause and effect. Nevertheless, when we compare the extreme body fixation in these media to the 70s' more carefree attitude towards body and nudity, it is clear that something has happened: Hardly a single young person today will shower together with others after gym class, and this is not only out of fear of being filmed and published for all the world. As described in the previous chapter, the very relationship to ourselves, our bodies, and the natural and cultural environments around us has radically changed – and seemingly not for the better. When a frightening number of girls believe they must operate on their labia to be able to show themselves naked to another person, it tells something about an externalization of the self-relationship that hardly leads us to genuine contact with the primal forces that humanity has always had potential access to.

Perhaps today's externalized, head-focused life and existence imply increased distance not only to the actual reality but also to our own body and the impulses and forces stirring deep within us. Forces and impulses that, in the absence of a meaning-forming framework, become frightening and anxiety-inducing rather than sources of power, direction, and joy in our lives. Thus, being seen naked entails something darker − something that awakens the horror over the unknown and incomprehensible as hinted at in the previous chapter. Perhaps, therefore, nudity today awakens a deeper anxiety than the more frivolous and lighthearted relationship previous generations seemed to have to this − even though it could also then be traumatic enough to be forced to shower together with both fellow students and teachers. In any case, humanity's relationship to itself and reality seems to have moved in the wrong direction − in such a way that it entails or corresponds with a multidimensional insecurity that seems to be more dangerous than the insecurity it has always entailed to grow up and find one's place in the world. It is against this backdrop we will attempt to answer what psychedelics are and how it can affect our relationship to ourselves and reality as such.

## Are psychedelics "narcotics"?

Before we delve deeper into the matter, it might be useful to get past the most superficial and least interesting answer to what psychedelics are − namely, whether they are "drugs" or not. The use of the term obscures more than it clarifies, confusing and bothering many. "Drugs" today evoke a certain set of associations: dangerous, illegal substances produced in dirty, makeshift laboratories in basements and outbuildings. We also think of addiction, human weakness, and immorality, destroyed lives, smuggling, dirty money, dealers lurking in parks and at street corners − and not least: criminal networks that stop at nothing in their quest for quick profit. Little could be further from the truth regarding psychedelic substances.

Etymologically, the term narcotics derives from the Greek word "narkotikos," meaning "numbing" or "sedating." Originally, it was used for agents that could induce narcosis or "deep sleep," and in a medical context, this first applied to opium, which is definitely both numbing and sedating. Psychedelics are not sedative in this sense, nor are cocaine, amphetamine, or other illegal stimulating substances for that matter.

Partly because of its imprecise meaning, "narcotics" today is only a legal term, not a medical or scientific one. In practice, this means that what is defined as "narcotics" changes in step with the substances authorities believe we should not have access to. This is concretized in the current "narcotics list" based on each country's Narcotics regulation and Medicine Acts. The narcotics regulation shall typically "determine what is narcotics," "prevent the spread and misuse of narcotics, including ensuring adequate control measures," and "ensure access to necessary medicines for medical and scientific use." For example, cocaine, as its harmful effects such as addiction, heart attack, and stroke became apparent, went from being an unregulated and popular substance added to everything from Coca Cola to red wine, to being listed among prohibited substances. This has not made the substance less sought after, but less "popular" in the sense that for most people, it can neither be acquired legally nor openly discussed without social consequences.

Cocaine was relatively new outside South America when it was introduced and thus has a short impact history in Western culture. It is therefore not very difficult for authorities to suppress its use to a level they can live with. When it comes to a substance like alcohol, which is also a very harmful substance when consumed in large quantities or over time, it is so closely intertwined with our culture that it is nearly impossible to imagine that well-meaning authorities could succeed in taking the beer away from Northern Europeans or Americans, or to crush the wine culture in countries like France or Italy. Alcohol is thus not likely to end up on any "narcotics list" anytime soon. The fact that this substance has its own law regulating production and sale, as well as several other laws imposing restrictions on its use, says something about the substance's strong cultural significance.

Legally, there is no doubt that psychedelic substances in most countries still fall under the term "narcotics" – simply because the authorities have decided that they should be. This is therefore also something that can be changed with a stroke of the pen if one were to agree on a change, and not something that is based on objective scientific criteria – such as, for example, the grouping of substances in the periodic system into gases, metals, etc.

The categorization of substances as narcotics also has a moral tinge, as the substances are seen as degrading for both society and the individual, somewhat akin to the prohibitions against homosexual practices we had earlier and which are still strictly enforced in, among other places, several African countries. Part of the argumentation against homosexuality was based on if men can have sex with men and women with women as they themselves desire, how can sexuality in a sufficient degree be directed towards the family and the continuation of the existing God-given social order? An interesting question is whether the power apparatus in the form of legislative politicians and the executive police in the future will be accorded as little honor for their restrictive attitude to psychedelic use as they today get for trying to control people's private lives by barging into the hidden gay clubs of the past.

Similarly, our relationship to the various substances is also based on a mix of religious moralism and utilitarian ethics: While alcohol use is closely intertwined with and to a certain extent compatible with working life as we know it, "narcotics" are seen as a threat to this way of organizing ourselves and the economy. Admittedly, the Friday beer can be harmful enough if it slides into weekend binge drinking, but in many people's world, it is an absolutely necessary reward for having endured five days in a row at work – regardless of whether the job itself is uninteresting or very interesting. Smoking a joint or doing some lines of cocaine has never become as closely intertwined with Western culture and the Protestant work ethic most of us are part of, voluntarily or involuntarily.

An ordinary person who has never tried psychedelics themselves – or made serious efforts to understand what it is – has absolutely no opportunity to think halfway clearly about the topic. At the same time, we should respect the police and customs authorities' work to prevent young or vulnerable people from out of ignorance, thrill-seeking, or social pressure consuming things they would not otherwise benefit from. A culture must be able to tolerate greater apparent paradoxes than this, if it is to be viable over time by opening up for personal and societal growth without panic-stricken setbacks against narrow-mindedness, intolerance, and stupidity; This applies whether this comes in the form of clowns on the political stage or contraction of our own minds and hearts.

Personally, I do not see that the community has the right to impose restrictions on adult individuals who wish to explore the nature of the mind and reality with these means. This naturally ties in with a much larger question of how we should organize good and fair societies, something we will look at more closely later in this book. Nevertheless, it must be said that I have considerably more faith in truthful enlightenment than in prohibitions and punishment as means to ensure safe, sensible, and meaningful use – so that as many as possible can make well-informed choices before they possibly choose to open the window that psychedelic substances constitute towards the deeper sides of human life and reality.

## Basic biochemistry

The most common answer to what psychedelics is, takes its starting point at the chemical explanation level – i.e., how molecules react with each other under different conditions. For substances a person can ingest or otherwise introduce into the body, the biochemical explanation becomes the most obvious: what happens in the organism when a given substance is introduced? When it comes to psychedelics, these effects are among the most powerful, strangest, and least understood effects on human consciousness one can possibly experience. It is so intense and special that it can hardly be overstated. No matter who you are or what you have experienced – including previous psychedelic experiences – a psychedelic journey can open up for phenomena and experiences completely impossible to imagine without having been there yourself.

Among the most "classic" psychedelic substances are primarily LSD and psilocybin, as well as mescaline, DMT, and 5-MeO-DMT. All these substances have very powerful effects that differ completely from what we are used to from "ordinary drugs." Over the last ten to fifteen years, we have learned a lot about how the substances interact with our central nervous system. For example, we believe to know that the psychedelic effects of psilocybin occur when serotonin 5-HT2A receptors are stimulated by psilocin, which is the residue after we uptake and metabolize psilocybin. The neurotransmitter serotonin is generally associated with happiness, joy, and well-being and also has significance for sleep, appetite, and memory. LSD also acts on the Dopamine D1-3 receptors, which may explain some of the experienced differences in effect. Dopamine is also a neurotransmitter, and affects mood, memory, pleasure sensation, motivation, arousal, and sleep – to mention some. Researchers at the University of North Carolina have also discovered that the LSD molecule appears to weave together with the receptors in a very intricate way. Part of the receptor simply lays itself right over the LSD molecule like a kind of lid, which is believed to explain the substance's long duration of action, up to 12-14 hours – against 4-6 hours for psilocybin, for example.

All this, belonging to the biochemical explanation level, is definitely very interesting and important, not least to uncover whether the substances can have dangerous effects that do not immediately manifest themselves during or right after use. The short answer to this question is "no." LSD and psilocybin have no significant effects on our physical well-being, neither acutely nor over time. They also have no tendency to create addiction – although psychological dependence is always a theoretical possibility regardless of the substance or phenomenon.

All this is well-documented stuff we will not spend much space on here. Several studies are ongoing, and numerous good books about the neuroscientific aspects of psychedelics have been published. With some exceptions, we will therefore leave the biochemical level and rather focus on the phenomenological – i.e., the effects as they appear both to the person taking the substance and to an external observer. The classification of the substances then, of course, also rests on these incredible effects, effects that make any comparison with other "narcotics" completely distant. This is not to say that one should not have great respect for psychedelic substances. Nonetheless, for most people, I would rather wish a difficult experience on psychedelics than a good experience on the "ordinary" substances on the "narcotics list." The reason for this, I hope, will become apparent in the coming chapters.

## How does it feel to be on a psychedelic trip?

The term "psychedelics" is derived from the Greek words *psyche* (soul or mind) and deloun (to manifest) – i.e., "mind-manifesting." Psychedelics or "mind manifesting" was first proposed by the British psychiatrist Humphry Osmond in 1957 and is better and more comprehensive than the name hallucinogen, which has also been used. This term implies that what one experiences are hallucinations without real value, which simply does not hold true – as long as the substances are used correctly. On the contrary, the particularly remarkable thing about psychedelic substances is, rather, that they let the mind manifest what is already there – i.e., conditions that in one way or another are important to the one experiencing them. This does not necessarily mean that what we might see or experience is a representation of things as they "actually are." Like most other things, it is more complicated than that.

As most people are aware, we are capable of producing images of the brain's activity and thus say something about where the various functions reside. The method fMRI, or Functional magnetic resonance imaging, visualizes blood flow internally in the brain in real-time and thus also how neural activation is distributed among the various areas. Regarding the effects of psychedelics, one of the most interesting fMRI findings is that these substances strongly reduce the activity in the brain's so-called *Default Mode Network*. This is the brain's "default mode" that keeps our daily notion of ourselves together in an apparent unity. The resting network is associated with memories and emotions, self-absorption, and what we might call "mental nagging" – all that just rolls and goes in our thoughts without there being any particular systematicity to the content. The study also showed that psilocybin causes stronger communication between parts of the brain that normally do not communicate much with each other. fMRI thus gives us, in other words, a visual representation of the substance's consciousness-expanding properties, something we will return to on several occasions through the next chapters. These are effects that to some extent persist also in the time after the psychedelic experience. Together, these phenomena are probably some of the mechanisms underlying the subjective psychedelic experience.

There is a very good reason why we talk about psychedelic "journeys" or "trips": In most cases, the effects are experienced precisely like that – as a journey. They offer a journey through the mind, body, our relations, the choices we have made, things we have gone through, and conditions that lie significantly deeper than this autobiographical level. For the person taking the substance, this is usually experienced extremely powerfully, and for a not so small share, the experience stands among the most meaningful experiences they have had in life. Quite illustratively, some have believed several years have passed as they are coming in for landing after such a journey and asked the tripsitter how they think it has gone with the family in the meantime.

Even though this time confusion for psilocybin's part typically passes within an hour after the journey, it says something about how far away from the superficial part of reality we move in and with these states. It also says something about that there is all reason to exercise great caution regarding where, when, and how we expose ourselves to such an experience.

## Set and Setting

Something that complicates and hampers the general understanding of and discussion around psychedelics is the fact that it is extremely important under which external conditions and in what mental state one takes these substances. Now, this is not entirely unknown when it comes to the world's most preferred intoxicant – alcohol. Most people who have made more than a few experiences with the substance know well that under certain conditions, it will only lead to confusion rather than the more relaxing and pleasant effect most are after. If one needs to concentrate – e.g., while driving or at work – almost everyone understands that a six-pack of beer is a poor preparation. If one is sad and down, for example as result of youthful lovesickness, the girls' night out usually does not turn into the lift one had hoped for but ends instead in snot and tears.

There are thus both external consequence hazards and inner emotional challenges with most substances that affect our consciousness – even for caffeine, humanity's preferred stimulating substance, there are limits to what is wise and responsible. For psychedelics, these effects are extreme. While alcohol loosens impulse control so that we end up doing things we would otherwise have opted out of as unwise, psychedelics, in the utmost consequence and in high doses, loosen up the very experience of who or even what we are – while we are completely present in the way that we neither sleep nor are unconscious as we otherwise know these states. In uncontrolled environments and without a certain preparation for what the effects can be, this can be demanding at a level few can imagine. It can therefore hardly be overestimated how vulnerable one can become. In an orderly setting, it can become one of the most rewarding experiences of life – in a less good setting something that resembles a waking nightmare one is convinced one can never come out of. This is not necessarily dangerous as such, and a normally robust person comes out well on the other side quite often also with personal growth as a result. However, mental immaturity, latent mental disorders, or simultaneous influence of other substances – which is often the case – can create unfortunate situations.

Unfortunately, the experience is that most people who try psychedelics do it the "wrong" way – i.e., the one that occasionally produces a classic "bad trip" event. The typical situation seems to be that a number of people – preferably quite "young and dumb" – gather to drink, smoke, and have fun. And in itself, there is nothing wrong with that. Maybe one of the party participants has taken mushrooms on a few occasions and introduces the others to the substance. Surprisingly often, despite the lack of good frames, it becomes a nice experience for the beginners – probably because the doses ingested in such situations are relatively low.

The fewer external frames we have to cling to along the way, such as walls, floors, ceilings, and other objects or people, the deeper we usually move into the experience. The external setting can thus by no means be randomly assembled. Even more important is the mindset we come to the journey with. Do we think this will just be fun and that we might see some funny colors – or do we already have a deeper understanding of what this can be? If we believe one always "melts together with the universe," tastes "divine love," or other large and positive feelings, we can also get quite a brutal surprise. Are we filled with everyday stress and obligations? Are we worried that what we are doing is illegal? All such bindings also affect how much we're able to surrender to what rises in us when the "control center" that governs what we perceive and do not perceive shuts down for a few hours. In addition, naturally, more bodily conditions also affect us. Have we been stressed for so long that it has settled as a fixed bodily mode we barely know we are in – maybe other than that we finally find some peace when we Friday evening collapse on the sofa after a few quick alcohol units?

Every individual thus comes to such an experience with their individual microcosm of thoughts, feelings, and experiences, tensions, neuroses, and psychosocial conditions that to some extent will determine what we can come to experience and in what order. This is precisely where the therapeutic and developing potential shows itself: Being shown or confronted with our own weaknesses – or strengths we did not know we had – in such an all-encompassing way can work both as merciless exposure therapy, powerful inspiration, and as reconstruction and integration of traumatic experiences of various kinds. It is thus not the case that psychedelic substances add "false happiness," peace, or distance to the problems in our lives – as many other substances tend to do. Rather the opposite.

It is not only stress and neuroses that hold us back from the psychedelic depths. The same does the quite ordinary and necessary programming we have all undergone from when we were quite small. What is a table and a chair, what are money, numbers, and words – and what do the words we use about various things and conditions mean? We have learned what "a meter" is, and we have concepts about computers, interior details, clothes, cars, buses, trains, bridges, and roads. "America" or "Europe" are also useful concepts that are nevertheless as good as meaningless when I am to approach the question of who I deeply am, what drives me, and which obstacles lie in the way for me to live as good and meaningful a life as possible.

All this practical and conceptual are necessary "scenery" for us to be able to function and unfold in the reality as we know it. Some are obviously also more important than other things: Our bodies, nature, and the conditions it sets up are not something we can or should abstract ourselves away from. This also shows in the way psychedelic journeys show us reality: At the "shallower levels," typically bodily and relational conditions as well as our relationship to nature and the biomass appear with a kind of "primary necessity" that feels extremely meaningful for the one in the psychedelic experience.

Things of more "secondary necessity," such as houses, jobs, and money, on the other hand, often appear as something that could have been very different from how we have actually arranged our lives. And not infrequently, we are shown how clinging to a given understanding of these "secondary things" is precisely what prevents us from changing our lives in a positive direction, take responsibility, and grow as people. Just as often, this seems to go hand in hand with a too distant and blunt relationship to the mentioned primary necessities – such as, for example, the previously mentioned relationship to body and nudity. Among the necessities of life are thus also our most important relations and the quality of these: if you prioritize achieving or confirming social status instead of spending some time with your old mother, children or your other real friends, this is something that can hit you like a slap in the face during a psychedelic journey.

Most of what in everyday life seems so important to give our lives frames we can function within – or a kind of scene to live on – thus becomes quite so unimportant. What we do at work, things we think we are interested in and concerned with, social media, clothes, or TV series mostly dissolve completely into the background. Instead, what forms and drives the one we actually or deeply are comes into focus. What is really important – or rather what would have been important for us if our lives were not filled with meaningless noise, anxiety, and unnecessary worries – can finally completely fill our consciousness.

## The First Experience

For those who have never had a psychedelic experience, talk about "things rising" in you, "being shown to you," or "letting go of" something may seem quite so distant – even though this in a more subtle form are processes that also happen in a normal unaffected state. So how is this actually experienced from within, quite concretely?

A common element in the typical first experience is a strong feeling of being connected with the surroundings or the universe. Perhaps it feels as if the boundaries between yourself and what is going on around are erased, and that part of what happens makes sense in ways you have never previously experienced. If you are sitting in a bath or swimming in the sea, it may feel as if you are all the water or that the water is you – something you, for that matter, can also experience if you are in bed with an eye mask and headphones on, as a trip "should" be carried out. If you are in a room with other people, you can feel a powerful connection to those present – or to all of humanity. For many, visual impressions also change in strange and fun ways, and it becomes difficult to determine whether the music in the room comes from the speakers or from your own head – or even if you are actually the music yourself. Perhaps you discover musical depths you never before have noticed, and if you close your eyes, fantastic colorful landscapes of figures and fractals usually appear – very similar to what we can see in psychedelic arts. At its best, this can be beautiful and quite so life-altering experiences, and many take with them this as something of the finest they have been part of without necessarily thinking that there is more to gain in this landscape.

My own first experience with psilocybin was as follows:

*After eating 15 grams of magic truffles from one of the Smartshops in Amsterdam, I went out again onto the street, sat down in the sun by the nearest canal, and waited for the effects. After a good half hour, I noticed that I sank more and more into myself, accompanied by a warm, rippling feeling. I had no great urge to open my eyes, but when I occasionally did, the impressions from outside felt overwhelming. Just by briefly looking at a perfectly average pretty woman, my whole body burst with pleasure so intense that it almost became unbearable.*

*After a while, I got up and went to a café nearby. I tried to eat some ice cream and waffle, but the sweet taste became too much. I therefore set course back to the tripping lounge at the Smartshop, a short walk that went surprisingly well despite the unfamiliar state of consciousness. As long as I focused outward and kept moving, I had sufficient control to navigate the cityscape. If I stopped and lingered, dwelling deeply, the experience intensified again.*

*Once inside the lounge, I settled down with my eyes closed and sat there for the next 3 hours. From a speaker came low, pleasant music, which seemed to give the experience even greater depth than it had had out on the street. (The effects of the psilocybin had naturally also set in stronger at this point. Typically, these intensify the first one and a half to two hours before it all culminates, and the experience changes character: From being intense and full of impressions, the whole often becomes typically more philosophical and wondering or even spiritual)*

*At the same time as the music in the room clearly affected me, another type of music also rose from the depths of myself. This was accompanied by strong visions of dancing African women in sensual rhythms that completely filled me. It was as if I myself was an active participant in a life-affirming primal dance while my body sat quietly on the sofa. This "inner music" had actually started already out on the street, so it was not the lounge music sneaking into me to then undergo some kind of psychedelic metamorphosis. It all arose somewhere inside me – or at least behind the sounds I actually perceived with my ears. (Even today, many years later, I can recall elements from this "performance" – complete with sound and images.)*

*Parallel to all this beautiful and pleasant, I also felt shame. Specifically, it was an embarrassment over being filled with precisely this beautiful and soft. In hindsight, I see precisely this spectrum between unrestrained well-being and shame as the most important thing I got out of this experience. For I too have room in me for beauty, softness, and uninhibited joie de vivre without there necessarily being anything shameful in this. Contrary to this, much of my individual learning from growing up, was that men should be solid workers and suppress any "weak" and soft that might pop up. Here, for the first time, I really became aware that I can spread my own being beyond this quite narrow room of possibilities. Even though I intellectually had long accepted that men must be allowed to encompass exactly what they want of feelings, it was something else to experience physically that I too am a much more complex ecosystem of gentle, soft, and positive feelings and sensations than what I had felt up to then. Without this contradicting being a "man" – or whatever labels one might need to stick on oneself.*

*Before I ate the truffles, I was quite tired and worn after the night before. I had had a few beers and also taken the opportunity to smoke a little marijuana at one of the Coffee Shops in Amsterdam. The result was that I did not fall asleep until 3- or 4 o'clock at night and actually felt quite shabby. Now it was as if I was completely awake and present in everything that happened, while I thus also became distant from the surroundings as soon as I kept my eyes closed, something I ended up doing in large parts of the about 4 hours the experience lasted.*

*During the last hour, the violent intensity gave way, and the vivid visual impressions inside my head disappeared. Instead, I felt an almost inconceivable clarity in thought and presence, not least considering how rotten my form had been earlier in the day. Even my clearest moments from life before completely paled against this.I now focused partly more on my surroundings, and instead of the powerful inner images in the first part of the journey, I could see how the pattern in the floor planks lived, breathed, and moved. Everything about the premises appeared beautiful and organic, and the people I saw were exclusively beautiful. Not in the near overwhelming and quite so erotically charged way I perceived them in the trip's initial phase but more as if a divine love ether permeated all living. In this phase, I also felt that I gained insights that appeared so important that I had to write them down to remember them later. All in all, it was a small shock to experience that what I had read about these experiences applied – also to me.*

*As the effects ebbed out, and I collected myself, I became aware that I was quite hungry. Along the way, the thought of food, drink, or other bodily needs had been completely absent. Certainly partly because of the dehydration in connection with the alcohol intake the night before, I also did not have to think about going to the toilet during the hours the trip lasted. On the other side of the canal lay an Argentine steakhouse, and the simple and certainly quite average meat dish I ate there was one of the most satisfying meals I have ever tasted. It felt as if every single bite nourished both body and soul. I drank a small bottle of beer with the food. It tasted good, but the alcohol did not contribute much, and I realized that I could just as well have drunk water without taking anything away from the food experience. My alcohol intake has never been either high or frequent, but this experience increased the awareness around the immediate negative effects of this substance so easily masked by the experienced positive. Like most others, I had always been aware of the uncomfortable "day after" effects, but physically realizing how quickly the poisoning effect actually sets in parallel with the intoxication we so gladly seek has forever taken away most of the interest in alcohol.*

*In addition to the confrontation with the mentioned shame, this was the most important lasting effect of my first experience with psilocybin. It is also an effect that has increased parallel with later experiences. After some of my journeys, I have for weeks or months almost felt disgust for alcohol and only after careful deliberation with myself have I taken it up again after some time – and only in selected situations.*

My first experience thus fits into a pattern many can recognize: Even though the conditions – set and setting – are not optimal, it very often becomes a nice and valuable experience. At the same time, there are both limitations and danger moments to this approach. Precisely because the substances offer such a powerful opening to "the land behind," such unskilled play is something one should not drag too far. In my many encounters with others who have made experiences with psilocybin or LSD – also in the role of "tripsitter" or "psychedelic guide" – I seem to see a pattern where the first experience for most appears to be relatively "gentle" unless they are explicitly in some very demanding situation or generally sit with massive repression of charged psychological material. As a main rule, it still goes well, especially if one has the opportunity to talk to someone afterward – someone who is not interested in condemning or explaining away what they have been through but who can help the person in question put it into a context that creates growth and expansion rather than fear and narrowing.

In the "orderly" settings I have been involved in, on the other hand, at least half of the travelers have more demanding, darker encounters with their inner world on their second journey. This also goes well in the sense that the situation remains manageable and not least that they usually come out on the other side a few neuroses lighter, a bit wiser, or more open to the world as it actually is rather than clinging to the most infantile ideas of how it should have been – ideas we all sit with whether we believe it or not. Very many have nevertheless been clear that it became a tougher encounter with themselves than they had thought and that they were glad they did it with someone present for them, and that they did not take a higher dose than what they actually did.

I took several new trips soon after the first, the first one already on the following day. This was a less remarkable experience. For one thing, it was only a day since the last time, which is too short for the resistance we build against the psychedelic effects to have completely let go. As a rule, it does not help to take more substance once the trip first approaches the end:

Little or nothing will happen. Also, the first few days after, the effect is quite so reduced. For another, the dose was only two-thirds of what I took the day before – only 10g of "magic truffles." Things definitely happened, and had this been my first trip, I would probably have thought it was great. Among other things, I experienced a kind of journey through time and space and strong identification with various human figures from epochs far ahead of our own time.

In this trip, I also tried to force contact with persons and conditions important to me without succeeding. I was a bit disappointed with this. All in all, it is easier said than done to force contact with what one wishes to contact, perhaps because it usually will contradict the inner logic and chronology both internally in and between each individual journey.

Some steering of the journeys is nevertheless not completely impossible. Many are surprised by how much control they actually have: they experience being able to choose between different themes, maneuver in various layers of their own psyche and body, and also to be able to refrain from entering things they see are important but which they perhaps at the moment do not feel ready to delve deeply into.

Having a clear notion of why one undertakes a psychedelic journey and thus also a kind of intention is also important. It is not that nothing important will happen if one does not have such an intention, but it ensures at least that one has actually thought through why one seeks a psychedelic experience. I always feel a little unease on the actual day: Is it right to do it today, and why am I actually doing it? Has it since my last journey become clear that certain themes need to be looked more closely at, or have I in one way or another strayed so far that more everyday methods do not bring me back on track? Or is it a type of escape driven by boredom or other restlessness?

There is not necessarily anything wrong with this, but having a relatively clear idea of why one chooses to undertake the journey is in any case important. In short: the greater awareness we enter into such an experience with, the more we can also get out of it – the clear opposite of doing it because the friends do it and believe it will just be fun. In the coming chapters, we will return to this from several angles and perspectives.

Several subsequent trips felt like treading water or being inside things I did not understand, even though I in retrospect see that I let go of tensions and themes that held me back both from deepening as such and from further personal development. The journeys were thus by no means without value. Still probably less came out of them than what could have been done if I earlier had begun to implement the methods for safe and meaningful use of psychedelics.

Admittedly, I had read much of the literature from the "wild west period" of the last century, but not really taken it in. At the same time, without these studies, I would have had considerably fewer hooks to hang my experiences on. Especially Stanislav Grof has done important and extensive work in categorizing different types of experiences and phenomenological levels the psychedelic experiences open up for. Most important to me, however, was to take in the importance of the mentioned set and setting – including the proper use of music. As I got more and more order on this, both the experience value and the utility value of my journeys increased.

## Paths the Trip Can Take

A psychedelic journey can manifest in several different ways, very roughly sorted into the sections below. It is not possible to determine for sure in advance which type of journey you will have, but through a series of experiences, most will experience all different aspects of these landscapes. Through a large number of client sessions, it has also become clear patterns that make it possible for us to have an idea of which direction your journeys will move in. Mostly everyone is surprised by how the experience actually manifests – both regarding theme and the structure of the experience.

In some journeys, you get very clear insights and experience that all of you, including body, feelings, mind, and soul, become completely "transparent." The same can happen with the relations to your closest ones, the world at large, or reality as such. So-called "oceanic consciousness" is often an important part of such an experience – i.e., the experience of complete boundlessness where one melts together with everything and everyone in the entire universe.

These experiences can come in several steps, for example, that one journey deals with your relationship to the entire biomass on earth while later journeys show the relationship to the more cosmic aspects of reality. In such an experience, the arbitrariness of our societal constructions becomes very clear, something that can dissolve both in locked thought structures and cemented notions of ourselves. Often one gains clear insights into measures one must take in one's own life regarding other people, job situation, life direction, or similar. It can also feel as if the mushroom or "spirit beings" show us some of the universe's deepest secrets, something that at its best can be completely life-altering. Often there is not very much to say or talk about after such a journey. What you possibly must do already stands clear for you, or everything has already "fallen into place" through an inner process that can be difficult to describe. It can still take time to integrate the greatness of the actual experience. Coming to terms with what is "objectively real" in these experiences and what is possibly symbolic often becomes part of this integration work.

We can also get an experience of being put "under the microscope." This is typically a quite demanding experience. Very often we are confronted with negative sides of ourselves. At lower doses, maybe the whole thing is experienced a bit from the outside, but still strongly. At larger doses, we completely merge with the experience of being "like that". We get things so straight in the face that we can no longer run from it. We can also completely merge with our less functional parts, such as anxiety, specific fear, memories from traumatic events, etc. At its best, this culminates and integrates with the rest of the self-feeling, so that we get rid of some of our "closed closets," and positive life energy is released.

Other times it feels as if the journey takes us to areas experienced to exist outside ourselves. This can also be quite demanding. Maybe we meet things we have kept at a distance or not wanted to see because they in one way or another are taboo for us. Maybe we try to "keep ourselves too good" to partake in certain feelings – for example, aggression or deep sexual forces. A balanced inner presupposes that we have a conscious relationship to all types of forces we can meet as humans – forces that reside in the large potentiality all living beings have access to. All unhealthy projection, distancing, and tabooing of these phenomena are unhealthy and something our inner healing force seems to tackle as soon as we give ourselves peace from the mentioned control center – the brain's resting network.

In such a journey, one can therefore well find oneself bathing in "the whole world's" rage, sorrow, pain, or misery – again precisely to be able to see, acknowledge, and thus settle down with that these are real forces we all partake in and that grab us under certain conditions. It is important to bring with you that what we experience here in no way is an expression of how "I deeply am," but that at the psychological level, it shows us what we as humans must accept and relate maturely to if we are to be able to develop further both as individuals and society. Luckily, it is not only bad or difficult areas we visit. Just as well, we get an experience of universal love that permeates absolutely everything. These are experiences that can be quite life-altering and redirect our lives in a positive direction.

We can also place the experiences along other axes: from the intrapsychic and quite concrete – such as, for example, your relationship to the job, partner, or alcohol – via the so-called perinatal – what is related to the fetus's experiences in the mother's womb – to the more archetypal and transpersonal, with large overlaps to the above-mentioned "areas outside ourselves." And while many experiences are very thematically oriented, the journeys often also become extremely bodily – perhaps especially on psilocybin. In such cases, it may be that we get released decades of stored tensions and that we even get rid of completely concrete pains or blockages we have struggled with either for good or for a time. At the same time, it is not always we manage to see or understand entirely what happens. We just know that it is important and that it often feels good afterward. In practice, we often experience a mix of everything described above, but not infrequently, the experience can be categorized according to these divisions.

It also occurs that the primary focus of the experience becomes the relationship between the traveler and the tripsitter. Then, the client will often experience regression or returning to earlier stages as well as various transference phenomena concerning the tripsitter – in other words, that the tripsitter's person evokes various feelings and reactions in the traveler, usually tied to the traveler's life themes.

## "Standard Experiences"

There is also a set of experiences that most who explore psychedelics over some time will have to go through. Examples of such are what we call *ego death* and the process of *death and rebirth*. Ego death is typically experienced by the one we believe and mean we are peeled away layer by layer until nothing other than the pure consciousness experience is left: the feeling of being present without being "anything" other than this presence. Personal history, family, body, gender, and all forms of identity are completely gone – the same with our surroundings. This can be experienced very demanding and typically raises the question, "am I then nothing?". Typically, this awakens our existential fear of annihilation, but as soon as we accept this possibility and surrender, we usually experience melting together with absolutely everything that is. The experience then completely changes character and becomes something very positive and pleasant. Many get a changed view of life after such an experience. Personal identity as such is also an important part of this since our connection to being in a male or female body, our ethnic and cultural background, sexual orientation, and worldview at large are very strongly interwoven with the view of who we are.

"Death and rebirth" is a type of experience that can give firsthand insights into the biomass's eternal round dance with death, decay, and transformation into new life. Some experience becoming subject to ritual sacrifices or gain deep insight into consciousness – the soul's – relationship to the perishable body and matter as such. Whether these experiences represent insight into real cosmic conditions or whether they are purely symbolic experiences, we will leav for you to decide, but as a tip to those who are thinking of undertaking such a journey, it is good to leave behind all preconceived ideas about how life and reality actually hang together – regardless of how well founded one might think these ideas are in science, religion, or everyday experience.

# Part 2

# Safe and meaningful use of psychedelics

*...it does not seem to be an exaggeration to say that psychedelics, used responsibly and with the necessary caution, can be for psychiatry what the microscope is for biology and medicine, or the telescope is for astronomy*
Stanislav Grof

Many stories are told about what one must and must not do while on a psychedelic trip, for example, that one must never look at oneself in the mirror. This is nonsense. What you should never do is take a psychedelic substance in a situation that is not safe enough for you to both look at yourself in the mirror and accept whatever feelings and impulses might arise. Both the internal experience of who and what you are and what you experience when looking at your own body can vary greatly from the everyday experience of yourself, and it should not be underestimated how demanding this can become – both during and afterwards. Precisely for this reason, safe, good frameworks and skilled guidance are essential.

Our aim is to create an understanding of the preparations and measures that are necessary for a psychedelic journey to take place in a safe manner and with the greatest possible benefit. The key here is to create conditions for an introspective experience where you allow yourself to meet your inner world with as much devotion as possible - without too many impulses to flee back into everyday reality.

As we have already discussed in the previous chapter, the so-called set and setting are important factors regardless of which consciousness-altering substance one takes. Even the effects of caffeine can take us completely by surprise and in the worst case start a cascade of anxiety and unrest that lasts for hours or days. In 2003, I was in Copenhagen with the rest of the philosophy students, which was my first encounter with coffee from a coffee bar. While the coffee I was used to at home did not cause me significant problems, this substance nearly knocked me down with severe inner unrest, and it also took a while before I connected it to the coffee. Since then, I have been very cautious about the situations in which I drink coffee or other caffeine-containing drinks.

Psychedelic substances cannot be compared with any other substance most people have experience with. The closest thing to potentially uncomfortable is probably the paranoia one can experience after smoking marijuana. This can be very uncomfortable, especially if the setting – the physical surroundings and situation – was not very safe to begin with. It's easy to get burned here. Environments one thinks one is safe in when sober can quickly reveal their true nature: outside of our control. The mindset in which we meet the situation is just as important, if not more so. If you have already experienced the paranoia marijuana can induce, at least it won't come as a shock if it happens again. At the same time, the fear of recurrence can also trigger a new difficult situation. And if you've been drunk and tearful a few times, you understand that this can happen again. Many also use this – consciously or unconsciously – as an opportunity to express emotions they otherwise dare not show to others. One of the positives with alcohol is precisely that there is a large social acceptance for expressing emotions that otherwise remain hidden. And often, it's exactly this we seek rather than the intoxicating feeling per se. Maybe we want to go to the Christmas party to see if something interesting can happen with the boss without having to fully account for it the next day – or precisely to create an excuse to leave the partner one already has. Or we know from experience that two glasses of wine make the conversation with a partner flow so much more easily.

We are thus not unfamiliar with actively using set and setting to achieve various effects when we intoxicate ourselves, even if people's awareness of this is relatively low. We are also not accustomed to the extreme effects psychedelics can bring forth, and without established social frameworks for the experiences, the risk of adverse outcomes is always greater. At the same time, it is not the case that an entire nation needs to possess an understanding of this. Subcultures can also do this job – like, for example, a spiritually interested group using psychedelics to achieve personal growth. Most people, however, do not belong to just such a subculture. They also have family, friends, and colleagues in other environments and, not least, the authorities – who typically try to combat what they consider to be unwanted drug behavior. Whether one shares the authorities' goals or not, they have the power and means to sanction anyone who breaks the laws in this area. A certain degree of secrecy, with the negative sides this can have, is thus also usually an unavoidable part of both set and setting in our part of the world.

The most obviously serious aspect of this is probably that the threshold for seeking help during or after difficult experiences becomes higher than it should be. Fortunately, this is something healthcare professionals are generally aware of, so they usually meet the individual with openness and warmth rather than moralism and condemnation. Those who are struggling during or after a psychedelic trip may not feel as confident about this. Will the parents find out? What about colleagues at work? And what about the employer? Moreover, even though healthcare professionals generally meet everyone with empathy and warmth, they might not have sufficient understanding of and experience with how psychedelics actually work to act as the helpful and catalytically releasing support they could have been - the kind that could turn a potential trauma into personal growth.

To this can be said that there also exists a more or less unconscious attitude in society that "illegal drug use" should not lead to positive changes. It is indisputable that this results in less interest in hearing about how psychedelic experiences have triggered positive processes, as the expectation for the last 40-50 years has been exactly the opposite: that this is something that makes you go insane. If someone in a polite company starts to explain how heroin saved them from alcoholism and changed their life for the better, it would likely create a rather awkward atmosphere around the table. And for the general public, healthcare professionals, and authorities, mushrooms and LSD have possibly appeared even more dangerous than opiates: as something that fries the brain and sends you straight to the mental hospital, in the worst case for the rest of your life. This is also how they have been classified on the drug list: as substances with great potential for harm, without medical value. Little could be further from the truth.

David Nutt shows in his book "Psychedelics" how the proportion of so-called "bad trips" correlates with the authorities' portrayal of psychedelics: in the most intense phases of the "war" against LSD in the late '60s and early '70s, the proportion of such experiences was considerably higher than in periods with less negative focus on the substance. If it's in the back of your mind that "LSD can fry your brain," it's clear that this fear could be activated and escalate during a trip that would otherwise have been normally challenging. Surrendering to the idea that "the brain is getting fried" is not something most people do voluntarily. Strong resistance to what is revealed during the journey is precisely what creates a "bad trip": the force from what is pressing on will be proportionally equal to the force we try to suppress it with. The moment we accept and surrender, what we feared typically disappears.

It's also negative that those who have had large and positively transformative experiences cannot openly talk about these, whether it's with family, friends, or colleagues. One of the most important things for us humans – to share and receive confirmation from others – is thus more accessible if one has been on a silent retreat and experienced gaining new power and direction from there, than for someone who has been on a psychedelic journey. When we see how much ideologically rooted fear and anger it evokes in people when someone says they have become vegans or have otherwise changed their diet, there's little reason to believe that telling about "illegal drug use" would be met with much openness and interest from the wider masses. Fortunately, this is now beginning to change, but much fear and many prejudices still linger - both among laypeople and professionals.


## Preparations for a Psychedelic Session

The practical preparations for a psychedelic journey should start at least a few days before it is actually to be undertaken, and preferably even longer in advance. The traveler must have decided or been informed about where the journey will take place. He also needs to feel confident that the location and room have the necessary qualities. This should not be something hastily arranged at the last minute – and it absolutely should not be left to chance.

The room must be a defined and comfortable space with immediate access to the facilities needed for a day and night's stay. Imagining a good hotel room is not a bad start if planning a place for a psychedelic journey: The room itself should be clean, neutral, warm, and inviting. It should also not be too large, the space itself appearing unmanageable. There must be windows, and the curtains should be thick and fully covering, so that it is easy to darken the room. The traveler should have access to a large and comfortable bed with pillows and blankets, and conditions must be such that one can stay in the room until the following day. There must also be sufficient space around the bed to move a bit if needed. A toilet must be located in close proximity to the bed, as it is in a hotel room, since it is best if the traveler does not have to leave the safe confines to satisfy their bodily needs at any point. Drinks and some snacks must also be available, and arrangements for a small meal after the journey is over should be made. A view from the room, especially of nature, is also beneficial. Even better is a terrace where one can stroll out into a secluded garden after the experience – if it feels right.

Mental preparations should start even earlier. Ideally, the psychedelic journey is something one has considered for a while. The traveler should feel deeply within oneself that this is something one truly wishes to embark on. There will almost always be a certain degree of excitement or nervousness before such an experience, even for experienced travelers. This is just how it is, and actually also as it should be: A certain seriousness should rest over such a situation. I myself am always a bit uneasy on the actual day. Often it manifests as a slight doubt about whether this is really the right day, and whether I have the right motives for going through with it: Do I have an intention, and does this match with previous journeys and where I now believe I have come in my own development? And not least, am I ready to surrender to where the journey will lead me, regardless of this intention? Because it is usually not as simple as knowing exactly where I am going, and the way there. On the contrary. If I knew how to reach my destination, I would simply walk there. Reality is that we both consciously and unconsciously hold quite cemented notions of how we and the world are and should be. These notions are of course also very useful, as they have kept us alive and brought us to the point we are at today. At the same time, it is these same notions and strategies that hold us back – that make the cobbler stick to his last rather than something completely different: letting go of a troubled past, a dysfunctional relationship, and limiting ideas of oneself.

Something that amplifies the difficulties we have with letting go is that we often inherit our notions from people we have trusted or depended on: parents, teachers, friends, idols, or religious figures. Thus, the issue not only revolve around our selves when we encounter the limits of who or what we thought we could be or do. Very often, it's about "deep programming" that keeps us locked in ideas of how we believe other people think we must be to deserve belonging, love, and other goods. To not be shameful outcasts without a place at the table. The fear of not belonging is so strong that even the slightest hint from those we depend on causes us to impose limitations on ourselves. Breaking these bonds has a price in the form of painful feelings, shame, or self-punishing behavior.

In this context, I cannot trust my own programming and the habits, feelings, and thoughts that spring from it. Nor, therefore, my own superficial maneuverability. Psychedelics offer an opening to the lands beyond all these limitations, and the key is to surrender to whatever may show itself. This should be an important part of our mental preparations. For the first-time traveler, it may help to adopt the same attitude as if going on a long overseas trip to a completely different part of the world, where it is obvious that everyday strategies are of little value. If you are to live a year with the indigenous people of the Amazon, it's best to adjust to the fact that they know better than you: When in Rome, do as the Romans. The vacation analogy is also valuable in that to a certain extent, we should have our "affairs in order" before setting out on a journey. It's hard to enjoy the vacation if at the same time we are brooding over unfinished work tasks and bills that should have been paid. Before a psychedelic journey, we must at least set aside things we think we should have done on that day and the next: calls we should have taken, tasks we should have done, thoughts we should have finished.

The point of these preparations is not to make the psychedelic journey a comfortable "peace & love" affair where no difficulties arise. Instead, the preparations should prepare us to meet what actually shows up. By clearing myself of everyday mental dross, I may be able to easier face whatever appears in front of me, and then enter it as best I can. The energy that otherwise goes to holding onto superficial, mental noise comes in handy when we visit areas and experience phenomena that lie entirely outside the experiences most of us have in life otherwise.

A psychedelic journey should also not start too late in the day. The traveler should be able to come back to themselves well before bedtime, so there is time to think through what has happened, or also, if necessary, distance themselves a bit from it. For psilocybin, this means that one should start no later than 3 PM, while an LSD journey should start as early as possible – preferably at 7 or 8 AM. It's good if all instructions are given the day before, so that on the actual day, it's just a matter of getting started – after some brief repetitions and reinforcements of what was discussed in the preparatory talks.

For the traveler, it may also be beneficial to be conscious of their own control mechanisms: Am I trying to steer the session by taking too much control over the setting, or can I surrender to the situation as it now is? It's fine and necessary to have a safe setting, but if the person setting out on a journey feels the need to control every minor detail, this may be an indication that more thorough mental preparations are in order. In the case of very inhibited behavior, body work and breathing exercises together with the guide or guides can be a good icebreaker. It breaks down some of the bodily resistance to free expression, as well as the social shame over "acting weird" in front of other people.

## Altered States of Consciousness

Most people have at some point experienced altered states of consciousness – primarily through various degrees of alcohol intoxication. Quite a few have also smoked marijuana or tried other drugs. Perhaps you also have tried meditation, or you have experienced unusual things at the borderlands between sleep and waking. Generally, the more conscious relationship you have to these states and their potential to create new thoughts and perspectives, the better prepared you are to curiously surrender and utilize the potential in a psychedelic journey.

Regarding drug experiences as such, these are states that typically add some kind of content from the outside: calm and relaxation on one side, or energy and alertness on the other. - Or false self-confidence. Psychedelics work rather by pulling aside a veil, allowing what already exists within us to come forward and become subject of conscious experience. Therefore, drug experiences as such do not necessarily prepare you for the psychedelic experience, or the potential that awaits within them. The key is the *conscious relationship* to the experiences: Who am I when I drink alcohol, daydream, or meditate? What comes forward, and what recedes into the background? At its best, this also prepares us for the fact that I am not my thoughts or emotions – but that there always exists an observing "I" that neither disappears, gets upset, nor becomes frightened. It simply is.

One of the special things about psychedelic experiences is precisely that consciousness, in terms of attention, is greatly enhanced, unlike, for example, alcohol, where we typically become less and less aware of what happens both in us and around us. Becoming familiar with the potential in altered states of consciousness is a matter of experience, and although one can have incredibly enlightening and life-changing experiences the first time one tries mushrooms or LSD, there is always more to learn about how we can utilize these states.


## The Music

Music – or another form of sound landscape – is extremely important for creating direction and securing progress in the psychedelic experience. Some researchers even claim that the music *is* the trip, while the substance is just the catalyst – what initiates the experience. This makes a certain amount of sense. Like the measures in the environment – such as having it dark and wearing blindfolds – music is also a means to direct attention inward, rather than towards insignificant things in the external environment. It should also create flow and evoke emotions. It should not *direct* the emotions, but rather resonate with tense strings inside you, where charged material lies. Therefore, the music does not need to be particularly advanced or "high-value" as a musician would rank it. Music that could accompany a cartoon works well: powerful and dramatic where it is demanding and scary, while striking much finer strings where more delicate matters are at the center.

We are in quite good touch with what kind of music that works well, and what does not. The playlist should simply correspond with the intensity of the phases the traveler moves through under influence of the substance: For the first 45 minutes or so after the effects have become noticeable, the music shouldn't be too dramatic. Light classical music works well at the beginning of this phase, while towards the end, a little more should begin to happen in the soundscape. As the transcenducing phase takes over, mysterious and interesting things should happen, having the potential to awaken a wide spectrum of emotions. Varying intensity and elements of ethnic rhythms work well here. It's okay to include a quieter piece or two, so the traveler has a chance to breathe out a moment on the way to higher and higher intensity.

After a total of 90 minutes to two hours, the effects of the substance are at their most intense, and then the music should also correspond with this: dramatic ethnic rhythms, symphonies, and overtures fit well. The music should not be scary, but build up and let go, then build up and let go again. Beethoven's Seventh Symphony is a good example – especially the more dramatic and powerful interpretations. Music from e.g. *Vangelis* also has sufficient drama, without being full of scary sounds as such.

After this culmination follows a phase often accompanied by clarity and insights. Here, like in the transcendent phase, interesting things should still happen in the soundscape, but the tendency over the next 45 minutes or so is for everything to begin to calm down towards something more meditative – which the playlist's next and final phase should consist exclusively of. Here, "cheap spa music" works well: the sound of waves or running water, bird chirping, wind, or other fine natural sounds are good.

The mentioned time indications fit well for journeys on psilocybin or MDMA, while the "descent" must be extended when using LSD. The first part up to and including the culmination is quite similar with these substances, while the last two phases last for hours on LSD. For my part, I often take LSD at seven in the morning, hence the culmination is passed well before lunchtime. Then I usually eat a light meal, after which I move from the bed or couch down to the floor, where I spend the hours until about 5 PM or so, still listening to music. Often, I get nice insights in these hours, related to the long lines of life, important relationships, and so on. Later, I often feel the need to call someone: family and friends, or perhaps renew a relationship I have neglected. Although one should generally be careful with calling people who do not know what one has been through, there may arise circumstances that make it right to contact someone other than the guide present. Not to make big decisions, but to be able to talk openly about things – which is usually a good thing.

As a general rule the music shouldn't contain understandable vocals, while it may include elements of chanting or singing in languages the traveler does not understand. Listening to vocal usage as such is a positive thing and can evoke powerful and healing reactions in the traveler. But as with the music in general, the intensity must be adjusted to the phase one is in, so that the traveler is not "held" longer than necessary in certain emotions or states. Here, a certain sensitivity from the psychedelic guide is also appropriate: if the traveler has been held very long in a certain state and does not seem to progress, changing the track can be useful. The same applies if it becomes obvious that the next track will be completely wrong based on what he or she seems to be going through. If the traveler expresses themselves emotionally or verbally along the way, it is naturally easier for the guide to get an intuitive understanding of which ongoing changes might need to be made. The experience here is to learn to trust the intuition, and not complicate it too much.

Music is thus important, but it shouldn't be a straitjacket. If the traveler feels it becomes too much having the music directly in their ears, this is okay. If he puts the headphones on the pillow, turn up the volume so that the music can be heard from the side. And if he throws them away, put on another speaker on the nightstand or somewhere else nearby. Many report that if they for a period didn't listen to music, it became a kind of parenthesis in the journey, something less comprehensible and more chaotic from which they derived less benefit. For example, many take off their headphones when they go to the bathroom. Encourage them in advance to keep them on also if they leave the bed or divan. As a general rule, the music should be on throughout the journey, unless the traveler needs to disconnect from the experience to ease the pressure or pull from what is happening. More on this later.

Occasionally, the traveler expresses a desire not to have music playing at all. This must be respected, as they are usually entering a state where they get a better grasp of what's happening without the music's guiding force. This happens relatively rarely, but that is exactly why it's important for the tripsitter to be particularly observant of individual variations. It's also important to note that this is primarily written with individual journeys on psilocybin or LSD in mind, based on a Western, "secular" setting. In a group setting with elements of ritual, significant deviations or variations from what is described here may be appropriate. This falls outside the scope of this part of the book, but it does not mean that these traditional approaches are not valid and important contributions to this field, also for the future. This applies even if they may seem alien to someone from a Western culture. The experience is that interest in this alternative and ritualistic aspect should arise within the individual, and not be imposed by the facilitator or facilitators of the journey. This also applies to interpreting what the traveler encounters on their journey: understanding should primarily arise within the traveler themselves. However, help with framing is often necessary, since much of what we experience contradicts our head-dominated understanding of reality, which for some can be summarized as believing that "nothing but what modern science has uncovered exists in the world," and that "I am my thoughts." The more cemented this belief, the greater the shock may be when the journey reveals that other realities are at least as real.

The primary needs of the guide or tripsitter must also be satisfied. The room must therefore have comfortable chairs sit in for 6 to 8 hours – or longer. If the sitter is uneasy, it's difficult to maintain the right attitude. The guide's state of mind is important, which also applies to regular therapists. However, a person under the influence of psychedelics may become so open and sensitive to their surroundings that any careless word, facial expression, or body language can lead the traveler down paths that are not necessarily productive. It's usually the case that whatever happens will in some way be related to the traveler's life and personality – and if not, to universally human themes. Nonetheless, allowing the experience to unfold primarily based on what arises in the traveler themselves, without external influences, is far preferable.

The contents and emotional state of the tripsitter are also important. Those who believe themselves fit to assist someone on a psychedelic journey must clear themselves of as much tension, emotionality, worries, rumination, opinions, and ideology as possible to maintain the greatest openness, empathy, and broad-spectrum love for the traveler. The sitter should not wish or want too much on behalf of the traveler and should not be too upset or moved by the person potentially having a hard time. One must also not let their own need for caretaking take precedence. Let such impulses simply pass and remain as neutral in your own inner world as possible; What's happening in the traveler is neither your business nor your process. Practice the same "emptiness" as in meditation: Let everything be as it is without engaging, analyzing, adding, or subtracting anything.

Especially when things get difficult, it's important to maintain this attitude. Typically, the traveler might momentarily pull up their mask to check if they are still in the physical reality, in a room with a ceiling, floor, and walls. This is often a way to cling on to the outer world, to not let oneself fall deeper than comfortable. But it can also be preparation for the opposite: a final check that one is safe, still where they were when the trip started, and that the person who said they would be there no matter what, is indeed still sitting there. Then, it's very unfortunate if this person exudes fear, or is caught in states concerning their own feelings. They should also not be too distracted, for example by reading a book, texting on the phone, or similar. This is not always wrong, and it's perfectly fine to make notes along the way, and perhaps check an email or similar, but one should not fall out of the open, neutral attitude. For example, disturbing news is something one should avoid. Wait with such until the session is concluded. If you notice the traveler turning outward, you should preferably leave the notebook or phone aside, and then note what you remember afterward, if you think it's necessary – and not just to play "good therapist." In such a context, it's even less about you than in a normal, therapeutic setting, and the apparent paradox is that the more you can keep yourself out of the way, the better job you do: The most important events happen in the traveler, and rarely spring from the guide's analyses or clever methods. When the journey itself is over and the traveler is back, it's okay to ask if you can take notes for later integration work.

When MDMA is used for therapeutic purposes, there will often be more interaction between the client and guide, often also physical. In "full dose" sessions on classic psychedelics, most of the interaction happens in the part of the journey where the person is returning to the ordinary state of mind, more available for such interaction than during the trip itself. In a variant of psychedelic therapy – *the psycholytic method* – the setting more closely resembles regular psychotherapy, enhanced by a smaller dose of psychedelic substance.

It sometimes happens that a person on a larger dose of psychedelics after some introspection no longer wishes to do that, turning outward towards the surroundings and the tripsitter. It's okay to tentatively encourage continued introspection, but as with music, the introspective focus should not be a straitjacket. Even though pure introspection seems to suit most who undertake a psychedelic journey, there are always exceptions. It seems that this need for outward contact is closely linked to personality, as the same person often has several such experiences one after another. Likely, there are issues within the person that need to be processed or overcome before they can surrender to greater, introspective depth.

Therefore, it's important to take the "here and now" seriously and join in the direction the traveler is moving – even if this means entering a more classical therapist role. It's not necessarily the case that one must become the person's therapist, but having a basic understanding of phenomena like transference and countertransference provides greater security in the situation: understanding what happens when the traveler plays out other, more important relationships in their encounter with you as a tripsitter, and that the feelings they evoke in you can also be important clues for the way forward. This is not something the tripsitter should "cleanse" themselves completely of: recognize that it's there, but don't let it take over, as it might if one is not conscious of what's going on in the situation. The degree of involvement along the way may end up being greater than expected, which is another reason to be well prepared, have physical and mental surplus, and plenty of time: this type of trips tends to last longer than usual – perhaps twice as long. My own experience is that journeys on LSD often have a communicative character towards the end, while with psilocybin, only three to four percent of my clients have primarily turned outward towards me.

Physical interaction may also be necessary on classic psychedelics, whether it's a hand to hold on to, a shoulder to lean on – or something more active from the sitter's side. This places great demands on the person. Perhaps a given level of physical involvement is required to avoid creating new rejection in a situation where the traveler is in an extremely vulnerable state of mind. Maybe the person needs to be held firmly, but lovingly. The balance of staying away, and letting the traveler be alone with what comes up can be challenging, as the therapist's own trigger points and blind spots can quickly become activated. The sitter's need to be important to the client, and to help, can also get in the way of the client's actual needs.

Because it's the individual's situation, personality, and background that lead the psychedelic journey, the sitter must be open to and prepared for anything. You might have been present for 100 travelers, and then something totally unexpected comes up. Hence, it's only the open emptiness that can accommodate whatever might arise – and no fixed ideology or schematic method. Suddenly, the traveler might decide to take off all their clothes to study their body like a two-year-old might, with all that entails. If you can't bear to be present in such a situation – and simultaneously understand that this in no way concerns your person or effort – you should not offer yourself as a tripsitter. You must not get ideas that it's your personality or effort that makes the traveler "safe" enough to express themselves freely – especially not on classic psychedelics. With MDMA, the relationship is often more important, but you should still continue to keep yourself – in the sense of your own issues – out of the equation, and neither contribute to sexualizing nor desexualizing such a situation. It simply is as it is.

Generally, it may be a good idea to keep your eyes closed for parts of the time when the traveler is outward-oriented or walking around the room, naked or not. You should open them now and then to show that you are present and available – and to try gauging whether it's right to "give" something more actively of yourself – but not to scrutinize or follow the traveler with your gaze. Practical assistance in the form of water, tissue paper, or similar is fine, but never, for example, offer the person something to "cover up with" because you yourself are uncomfortable with a situation where he or she is lightly dressed or naked. It must happen only in response to an actual need from the traveler, or as a very subtle gesture the traveler barely notices. Never should it be such that the traveler gets the feeling that they "should" cover up, wipe off, or in any other way make the situation more comfortable for the tripsitter. Such feelings may arise in the traveler because they are relevant to him or her, but it should never be the tripsitter who creates and transfers them to the traveler.

The one thing that must never happen in such a situation is active, sexual involvement from the tripsitter's side. There can be difficult boundary situations where the traveler needs physical contact or reassurance, something that must never lead to one actively touching the person journeying in a sexual way. It's somewhat the same as in a situation where, as parents in a naked or lightly dressed state, you play with small children: You should position yourself so that the child doesn't start to play with the adult's genitals – while also avoiding any subtle conveyance that the genitals themselves are "dirty" or in any way something to be ashamed of.

The rule of not bringing your sexuality into the equation may very often be valid also when you sit for a partner, and it requires great care and experience from both parties to understand when sex is appropriate, and when it is not. Generally, on low dosages and for experienced travelers, it may be perfectly fine. When the opposite is the case, it is usually not a good idea to engage in sexual activity.

There might also be situations where active, physical intervention from the tripsitter's side becomes necessary, for example, if the traveler decides to do something dangerous to themselves. It is absolutely not the experience that such things happen, and generally, the setting must also be safe enough that such things *cannot* occur. For example, it's unnecessary to place the session in a room with a balcony high above the ground, where the "pull" from humans' inherent fear of heights can take hold of the traveler and make such fear or other "death drives" a theme. Not having dangerous objects lying around, such as knives or objects that can appear as weapons, must also be obvious.

As a tripsitter, I prefer not to have other plans for the day in question, and preferably not early the next day either, so I don't have to worry about whether I will make my later appointment, have time to prepare for the next client, or similar. I also strive not to be a tripsitter two days in a row, both to avoid worrying about making the appointment, and to have time for myself between sessions. Although most psilocybin journeys are over after 4-6 hours, it's not uncommon for the entire session, everything included, to last 10-12 hours or more – and in a few cases, it has happened that I have spent the night in the same room as the traveler. The most important thing is that the atmosphere is characterized by having "all the time in the world." For my part, the slightest hint of being tied to something outside the room where the session takes place ruins the open and vacant attitude necessary to do as good a job as possible. Naturally, this can be solved by being two or more tripsitters, which also creates greater flexibility in case something happens at the home of the sitter. The traveler cannot be left alone no matter what happens: Even if your country is invaded and cities burn, you must still sit your post until the journey is well and truly over, as long as nothing physically threatens to endanger the traveler and yourself. You should think carefully about the implications of this before agreeing to help someone maintain the space during a psychedelic journey. Your own needs must always give way, no matter how urgent they may feel.

Towards the end of the journey, it is most often the traveler themselves who expresses that it's enough for now. Either it's simply over, or the person is tired and full of impressions and wants to return to the surface. The traveler usually takes off the mask and headphones on their own initiative, while the sitter may well ask if it's soon time to turn on or let some light in the room. This should be done gradually, so the light isn't bothersome.

As the experience comes to an end, and the traveler again turns their focus outward, it's still important for the sitter to hold back. Don't ask too much at first. Let the traveler begin to tell. Don't fear the awkward silence – it's only awkward for you. Inside the person who has been on the journey, things typically continue to happen: new associations form, feelings land, and experiences are digested. You as a tripsitter or guide don't *necessarily* have a big place in this, unless the traveler invites to it. Maintain the open and vacant attitude, and don't be misled into thinking that you can now have a completely normal conversation. As the hours pass, the more normal the conversation can become, but it must still happen on the traveler's terms; Not to satisfy your curiosity, for you to be a "good therapist," or other irrelevant matters.

The same applies if the traveler prefers to be alone. Respect this, withdraw with reference to the agreement to make contact, for example, the day after. You should also clearly express that he or she can contact you at any time during the next day or so, and that you will also be available for questions and conversation later. Make the agreement for a follow-up conversation already before the trip starts, then confirm it before you part ways.

# Closing instructions

Everything mentioned above should naturally be part of the preparations for a psychedelic journey, whether it's you who will be embarking on the journey, or if you are to create the space and guide others. In addition, some final instructions should be given to reinforce the already prepared mode or mindset, and to ensure that the individual has the right tools for their journey.

Traditionally, it has been common practice to send those embarking on life's final journey with various artifacts. Everything from the ancient Egyptians to the Vikings were accompanied by different objects into their graves, which the survivors assumed the deceased would need in the afterlife. Typically, these were jewelry, combs, ointments, spices, or weapons. Some of the wealthiest were also known to take horses, slaves, or even entire ships with them. And it wasn't far-fetched to think that what the deceased might need in the afterlife would be the same objects that had been useful in their corporeal life. Someone setting out on a psychedelic journey – especially on a high dose – must be prepared for an experience completely different from anything they have previously encountered, not unlike relinquishing life and surrendering to the eternal hunting grounds beyond. Hence the comparison with grave goods. For also on a psychedelic journey, it turns out that essentially the same mental, physical, and spiritual tools you would use in everyday life are what you'll need. At the same time, for most of us, everyday life has untaught us the necessary contact with a good self-understanding and the most important tools for adjusting internal states; the potentially powerful stories about ourselves have been replaced with an inferior, technical self-understanding, and the best tools have been replaced with an excessive belief in rationality – with a neuroscientific and diagnostic mindset as the spearhead of this.

A psychedelic journey often re-establishes contact both with a richer self-understanding and the tools we need for adjusting our own, internal states. Often, it feels as if the psychedelic substance – and perhaps especially psilocybin – offers us a "helping hand" along the way. Many describe this as if a kind of loving presence of the mushroom, various spirits, or even God, speaks to us and helps us find the way. However, this presence might just as well grab you by the scruff of the neck and brutally make you face down into the remnants of the life lived. It can thus be tough love, but from the perspective of the traveler, it also most often feels as if there is "something" in the substance or "out there" that only wants what's best for us.

Some say it feels as if the mushroom scans their body and emotions before starting various types of work where it's needed. No matter what happens, it's important to surrender to this as much as possible, rather than trying to steer and analyze. Trust and acceptance are key words here, as opposed to fear and the need for control, which humans are usually greatly governed by. Since most of us are so disconnected from the trust in these archaic forces, we should thus provide the traveler with some simple instructions on how to encounter this, whether it's through the body, thoughts, or other aspects of ourselves.

## Managing expectations

It's also important to manage expectations: It's understandable that many feel they "deserve" a good and enlightening psychedelic journey after a life of difficulties, but it doesn't work that way. More often, the opposite is true: the more challenging one's life has been, the tougher the experiences they may need to navigate during psychedelic exploration. This is a nuanced rebuttal to the critique that psychedelics are a "shortcut": yes, psychedelics will typically accelerate personal development compared to conventional psychotherapy or self-improvement methods. However, the ordeal one might go through can be more intense than most would choose if they fully understood the potential extremities of the experience. It's precisely this willingness to confront extreme discomfort that is necessary for true progression, rather than merely glossing over issues – a choice that must be respected as legitimate for some individuals. Optimal engagement with psychedelics should emerge from within as a compelling desire to explore beyond the superficial rim of our existence.

Expectations for what can be achieved in a single session should also be moderated. It's very common for the journey to move in completely other directions than anticipated. Therefore, an attitude of openness – allowing whatever emerges without judgment, escape, or attempts to steer in a different direction – is beneficial. Often, the themes that surface are essential for moving toward one's initial goals. Moreover, it's crucial to remember that while some journeys result in profound healing on their own terms, they are typically parts of a longer personal development process.

It's also crucial to inform the traveler about the typical onset effects of the substance being used. For LSD, effects usually begin around 40 minutes after ingestion, while for ground psilocybin mushrooms mixed with citric acid, effects can start within 20 to 25 minutes. During this initial period, the traveler should direct their attention inward and prepare on the bed or couch where the main part of the journey will take place. Eye masks and headphones should be ready to be put to use as soon as the effects start to manifest, with the trip sitter controlling the music from their device. The traveler should not need to interact with this technology themselves. The traveler's phone should be turned off or set to airplane mode. Of course the sitter's phone should also have silent alerts only, and at no point should the sitter make or accept a call.


## First onset of the psychedelic effects

The first signs of the psychedelic substance hitting often include tingling in the fingers, a sensation of waviness in the body, or visual disturbances. Some may start seeing colors or shapes, especially with closed eyes. A feeling of coldness or warmth – or both – is not uncommon. As soon as there is no doubt the psychedelic effects have appeared, putting on the eye mask and headphones helps the traveler avoid the confusion of having to deal with both internal and external inputs. By surrendering to the music and the unfolding experiences in both body and psyche, the journey will take the individual where they need to go. Sometimes, resistance to this surrender can manifest as nausea, discomfort, pains, or various types of anxiety. Especially when the traveler has a rigid personality style, scores high on anxiety – or both, as is very often the case – this difficult onset-effects may occur.

Typically, those who have a lot of fear about their physical states may find the entry phase challenging: if someone has previously rushed to the emergency room with panic attacks and fear of heart attacks but is otherwise physically healthy, a difficult entry into the psychedelic experience is very likely. It's important to communicate this clearly to the traveler along with assurances that such reactions are not dangerous with substances like psilocybin or LSD. Equally important is to actively offer various methods to handle any discomfort: one should not just lie still and try to endure. Instead, one should move the body intuitively "with" and "against" any discomfort, and even amplify what lies there: after decades of covering up the body's need for "emotional acting out," it often requires help to initiate the processes that should naturally occur. Breathing into, rather than away from, the uncomfortable feelings is advised.

If there's concern that anxiety or a rigid and inhibited personality will create problems, the trip sitter might suggest starting the session with joint "bodywork": in the time before or right after the substance is taken, those in the room together can perform various stretching exercises focused on letting the go of bodily defenses. This also helps release some of the potential shame of "acting out" while another person observes – and perhaps even takes notes on what's happening. Be more proactive than usual in offering a hand to the person embarking on the journey. Sit a little closer than usual and extend your hand as a gesture of support. In such cases you may even offer a slight initial touch to test the response of the traveler.

As the journey commences, various mundane topics, thoughts, or images related to recent conversations, things you've been thinking about in the last few days, or other matters that have crossed your attention may come up. Sometimes we may get caught up in these, either positively or negatively. It often serves little purpose to actively pursue these images or concepts to any great extent – just let them pass. On the other hand, we should not resist them either. A person I was trip-sitting for told me after the journey that in the beginning, a sort of sign appeared before the eyes, highlighting some concept we had discussed in the preparatory conversation. This concept felt totally irrelevant, and the first impulse was to try to push it away. What happened next was that the "sign" came much closer and filled more of the inner visual field. Fortunately, the traveler remembered what we had discussed: that absolutely everything that comes up must be accepted and embraced. The moment they told themselves, "If it's going to be about this, then so be it," the sign moved to the periphery.

This is typical: What is not actually important shows itself and passes without further ado as long as we neither resist nor get too caught up in it, whether out of curiosity or other reasons. Where the topic truly matters to us, this will be made clear by the emotional charge felt in the body. You may feel resistance or fear approaching the topic, or it may evoke other difficult feelings or thematic associations. The path is always to accept, embrace what you are shown unconditionally, and through this – let go completely. Trusting that this process will unfold as it should is important: trust that you will carry something important away from the experience without trying to control it, and trust that there is light and goodness behind everything that feels dark and challenging.

Trust in the process also means trusting that you will not "go mad". Often, it's the fear of going mad that causes us to fight against what we are shown rather than what we are shown per se. Society's low level of understanding of the psychedelic process does more harm than good: If you've heard that psychedelics can make you psychotic, fear of going mad may very well trigger a difficult experience. The mechanism here is that we fight against what is revealed to us. The underlying force will push back with equal intensity. It's always our own struggle against seeing, accepting, dissolving, and letting go that creates perceived pain and difficulty. The world just is as it is. Probably, everything is always there, completely accessible to us, but our programming, neuroses, and tensions prevent us from seeing it. If we can fully accept what we are experiencing – bear to let the world show itself raw and unfiltered for a few moments – we can make significant progress.

In practice, this means accepting everything you might see, feel, hear, or otherwise experience, even if it feels difficult, strange, painful, wrong, disgusting, or out of place. Meet it with as much curiosity as possible, knowing you will come out of the experience intact, just a bit wiser and more balanced than before. Throughout the journey, as mentioned, many feel guided by something deep within themselves or something greater than themselves. The experience is that it's right to trust this, even where specific messages about various matters are given. Fully trust that the process is already leading to something good.

As mentioned, we often have clear expectations about the direction the journey should take. More often than not, the journey takes a completely different path, and any idea that it wasn't supposed to be this way will manifest as resistance to what actually comes. If it had been so simple that we knew the paths we must take to find the answers within us, we might not need to take psychedelics – or engage in therapy and self-improvement at all. Our outer layers of consciousness do not know the labyrinth we must navigate to find what we seek, and rationality *almost always* hampers this more than it helps. Therefore, do not attempt to analyze during the journey. Just let it be as it is. You can analyze it later. It's also good to remind that the journey typically will have recognizable phases, as described in the section on music. And it is appropriate to prepare the traveler for the fact that the exit – the last hour or hours afterward can be difficult if one has traveled far from his or her usual level of functioning and consciousness, especially on high doses.

Particularly where anxiety is the issue, the transition back to regular consciousness can be tougher than the traveler might expect. A similar phenomenon can occur with deep depression: Even though the journey itself may have a very positive angle, it's not unusual to be fully confronted with one's most depressive sides, often as one is coming out of the journey. This typically passes within a few hours after the journey has ended, but if the traveler is in a life situation that cannot easily be changed, it's common to further open up to the seriousness of this situation, which will often be felt both positively and negatively in the days and weeks following the journey.

At some point – typically at the beginning or around the middle of the journey – it may also happen that the traveler feels things are getting heavier than they are ready to receive. Although the very best usually is to dive into and through the difficult material, where it typically will culminate and transform into something positive, it must be up to each individual to decide how much they're willing to engage with what comes up, including potential discomfort, fear, or resistance.

Many will intuitively lift their eye mask and look around the room as if to anchor themselves to the external, everyday reality. Often, this is sufficient for the individual to surrender anew. Other times, the traveler needs to talk a bit with the tripsitter. Often, the pull from the topic or phenomenon diminishes after a 20 to 30-minute conversation, and the traveler can again enter the journey on their own. All measures to enhance introspection can thus be reversed to relieve the pressure or pull from the psychedelic experience: the eye mask can be removed, the music moved further away or turned off completely, the curtains opened, and the lights turned on. In cases of very strong anxiety that prevents deepening, stronger measures can be used: take a walk, eat a meal, or do other everyday grounding activities – along with continuous reassurance that these are entirely normal reactions, and that there is now so and so long left until the effects of the substance wear off, and everything returns to normal. In one case, at the traveler's request, I also dialed emergency services on the phone – without actually pressing the call button – before we talked it all through by focusing on the fact that the breath and pulse were actually completely normal: After talking for five minutes, it became clear to the traveler that there was no real lack of air, and that it was unnecessary to go to the emergency room.


## The dose

Regarding the size of the dose, this is finally agreed upon in the hours before the substance is taken – unless it's a standardized setup with already predetermined doses. The traveler should have thought about where they want to "land" in the time leading up to the particular day. Is this a first dip into the psychedelic landscape, or is the goal to blow all gates wide open? Even though it is ultimately up to the traveler themselves to decide the goal, the decision should be informed, and not based on loose assumptions and anecdotes from "party trippers".

Broadly speaking, the experience is that low to medium doses primarily open psychological doors, while very high doses "open the gates to the cosmos". By low doses, I mean anything under two grams of dried Psilocybe Cubensis – roughly equivalent to 20mg of pure psilocybin. By a medium dose, I mean two to three grams, while anything over three grams is a quite high dose. Naturally, there is also a world of difference between four and six grams, so this is just a preliminary rough division, primarily with the inexperienced in mind. Many official studies also work with doses between 20 and 30 mg of psilocybin, so in this sense, one is also on safe ground starting out in this area – of course provided in an orderly setting, as described here. If the traveler has a lot of anxiety and is perhaps also unsure about the setting itself, two grams or a little less may be a good starting point. If there's no such anxiety and unrest in the picture, 3 grams or even slightly more may be a good starting point.

As things begins to happen, we put on the eye mask and headphones with the pre-selected music playlist. Then, it's important for the tripsitter to observe the situation. How is the breathing? Is the body tensing or locking in a way that suggests the traveler is holding back and not able to dive into the experience – or doesn't anything seem to happen at all? If the individual seems to be struggling a lot with letting go, it's good to touch them on the shoulder (or another pre-agreed part of the body) and ask how things are going. If it's difficult to get into the journey, encourage the use of the body, as you have already discussed. Sometimes it may also be appropriate to increase the dose, as most people seem to have a kind of threshold where they are neither tripping nor unaffected – a place that is often not so comfortable, without much gain is made from being in this discomfort either. It can also be helpful to talk about the anxiety or discomfort for 20-30 minutes before again encouraging entry through the body and emotions. Once the individual is well into the experience, it is common for them to yawn several times. This is not a sign that they are bored or falling asleep but, on the contrary, that they are well on their way.

Up to two to three hours after the journey has begun, it's possible to take more of the substance, and thus go deeper. Often, it's the traveler themselves who realizes that more is needed. Experience shows that there is all reason to trust their intuitions. Perhaps it feels as though a theme lies just out of reach – something that feels quite physical: as if we can't quite stretch far enough to reach it. A booster dose will usually enable us to get to where we need to be. Maybe I'm already inside something important and difficult, but after circling around for a while without being able to resolve or let go, it becomes clear that I need a refill to be able to release the charges existing there. Another situation is when nothing is happening at all. Then it's good to increase the dose by 50%, and see what happens. If this sparks something, but still not sufficiently, one can increase the dose in steps of one gram. Since neither psilocybin nor LSD is harmful to the organism, this is completely safe.

It's also not the case that dosing needs to be adjusted for body weight, muscle mass, gender, or similar. It seems to be exclusively personality and personal history that determines how high the dose needs to be to have an effect: While rigid personality types typically require higher dosing, sensitive souls can have very powerful journeys on two grams or less. The highest dose I have been involved in administering is ten grams. Even then, the journey wasn't anything spectacular – less than what two grams do for a sensitive person. Oddly enough, the individual's spouse also ended up at the same dose, even though the starting point was different: for one, the individual was on SSRI antidepressants, which often entails that the dose needs to be increased by as much as 30-50%. Secondly, the desired landing spot was of a spiritual nature: the individual wanted as much contact with the spiritual reality as possible – something that happened.

Here it's important to understand that having had a great cosmic and spiritual experience doesn't necessarily mean that one has let go of all everyday neuroses. For some, such experiences can also lead to some kind of "spiritual bypass", meaning that one believes to be "more evolved" than what is the case. Perhaps the individual has an excessive focus on the spiritual, "God's will," or similar, while everyday life and relationships suffer because of this. It's not uncommon for religious individuals to struggle with this, not least in the sexual domain: Perhaps one believes oneself to have "transcended" such basic things as body and sexuality, while the reality is that the distorted relationship to this important part of life blocks both a good daily life and further spiritual development.

If we become aware of such conditions either in ourselves or in someone we help through a psychedelic experience, much can be gained from attempting some journeys on low or medium doses either before or between the higher doses. At its best, this allows us to work through precisely those layers we might otherwise skip over. What we also see is that as bodily and emotional conditions are processed through a series of journeys on medium doses, later journeys open more and more to spiritual experiences – even though the doses are not increased. This is also something pioneer psychonaut and therapist Stanislav Grof noticed and commented on in his writings.

Learning to journey consciously into the psychedelic landscape, rather than hitting it with very high doses dead on, has several advantages. Firstly, nothing is lost by taking the journey step by step – possibly other than the sheer novelty and fascination. There lies a certain learning, both for meditative or psychedelic deepening and for everyday life in stretching towards what lies beneath the surface, rather than being dragged there by the neck. Gradually identifying levels of fear and other resistance rather than being pulled straight through also has its merits.

Regardless of dose or goal – receiving instructions on how such resistance can manifest is also useful. Sometimes, it doesn't seem as if much important or relevant is happening even a good way into the journey. Perhaps there are just funny colors and fractals churning and tumbling around in your inner vision, but no emotions, themes, or merging with something greater comes up. One natural solution to this is to increase the dose, but it can be equally useful to scan through the body, emotions, and thoughts to find where you're holding yourself back. Regardless of the dose, the traveler should first try to identify which thoughts, feelings, or tensions might be preventing further deepening. Often, there are self-critical thoughts like "this probably won't work for me," that you look silly lying there, or that it's uncomfortable, useless, or otherwise a waste of time. Try to let go of such thoughts, and instead feel what exists in the body or the emotions. If the colors or figures are amusing or fascinating, you should also try to let go of thoughts about this. Just let it be. The colors and figures are rarely important.

David Nutt describes in his book "Psychedelics" how patterns and geometrical figures seem to represent the "primordial forms" of what later becomes visual impressions we can understand. Experiments on frog brains have shown that precisely such geometric figures are some of the first to form in the newborn. Perhaps, then, on a first journey, we see this phenomenon for the first time since we were babies – although we can also experience it in a weaker form, for example, between sleep and wakefulness. Regardless, it seldom makes sense to focus on these figures. Rather, direct the inner gaze "behind" – towards your inner horizon.

The body and emotions, on the other hand, are very important clues: perhaps you notice a tension in an arm, in your neck, or in the fingers. Simply focus on this, but don't try desperately to relax. Instead, tense the relevant area even more, and then relax. Do this several times, and then see if the tension has released. Perhaps you also feel an urge to make certain movements with the relevant body part. Allow this to happen without resistance, and even enhance the movements, as we have already discussed. Then let the body part rest a bit, then try again if more tensions still reside there. Perhaps now another body part calls, where you can initiate a similar process.

Here it's important not to use thought to keep the focus fixed on something you could have let go of. Doing so creates a sort of "floor" to how deep the experience can lead you. Identify tensions, work a bit with them, and then try to let go – as a purely physical event. Often, it's also the breath that "holds back". Perhaps it has temporarily stopped, and you become fascinated by not feeling any lack of air – or the breathing pattern is inhibited. Recognize this, try to breathe a bit deeper and more rhythmically than normal, and then let go. Then forget your breath, as long as there's no more "natural energy" there.

Sometimes, the breath or other bodily conditions fill the entire trip, or large parts of it. If that's how it's supposed to be, then so be it, but as mentioned, try to feel if it's actually you yourself holding onto the purely bodily aspect. Typically, the most is gotten out of the trip by quickly letting go of such minutiae – tensions where there's no emotional charge or clear themes becoming apparent parallel to the experience of the bodily tension. Perhaps it's only after a couple of hours that the inner landscape opens wide, and themes and emotions potentially become clear and find their resolution. Perhaps, as mentioned, one could have gotten there by increasing the dose, but then one might have found a different thematic landing spot for the journey. This is, of course, difficult to verify, as each individual journey is what it is, partly based on the work that has been done previously. Regardless, the aforementioned awareness of one's own tensions and resistance can help us go further and deeper.

Regarding follow-up sessions, my experience is that these are in at least half the cases more demanding than the first round. It can therefore be a good idea to reduce the dose for a second journey – at least compared to what became the final dose in the first round. Check in after 30 to 40 minutes, and if it's already dark, challenging, or difficult in some other way, it's not necessary to add more – unless the traveler themselves feels that this is needed to break through some layer or shell to move forward.


## Integration

We must say a bit about how we specifically can help ourselves and others towards greater understanding, better health, and personal growth during or after a psychedelic experience. For the vast majority who take psychedelics in an orderly setting – including the preparations we've described above – much of this falls into place by itself either during the journey itself or within a week after the journey.

What happens on such journeys is often an integrating and re-associating process in itself. As long as one does not open too many psychological and spiritual doors at the same time, making it impossible to do even preliminary integration during the hours the journey lasts, the process often unfolds in a way that one goes through various bodily and emotional charges, while the thematic becomes clearer and clearer. Sometimes, the anxiety or discomfort in these charges comes first in the journey, and the insights towards the end. Other times, several journeys are required before the insights appear, and both the bodily, emotional, and cognitive levels are integrated. The process is exactly the same as in, for example, Reconstruction and Integration of Traumatic Stress treatment, but often occurs without external help: in some way, psychedelics – perhaps especially psilocybin – enable us to let our own, inner healing power take more or less full control for a few hours, while the process continues in a milder form for several days after the journey.

We know this both from experience and through studies like fMRI: Even several weeks later, the brain's internal communication is noticeably different and "richer" than before the journey. At the experienced level, thoughts and feelings often emerge in the days after the journey – sometimes as flashes or recollections of the experience itself. Personally, I can have a kind of "film" from elements of the journey played back by talking with other people about my experience. This is a fine and useful process, even if it is exactly what many would describe as "flashbacks" after a weakly planned and poorly executed journey. If the journey was marked by panic and resistance against what wants to surface, the remnants will be more and numerous and perceived as scarier in the days afterwards – precisely because one dwells in resistance to the material, and preferably doesn't want anything to do with it.

It's our anxieties, tensions, neuroses, and various ideological conditions that keep this material and these charges in place where they have become stuck, while psychedelic substances initiate a process where it all comes into motion, and to lesser greater degree is released. What is often called a "psychosis" in individuals who have had an unprepared and poorly managed psychedelic experience, is nothing but this material that has been set in motion, pressing to find its way to the surface. As long as there's no predisposition for schizophrenia – in which case one should never have taken psychedelics in the first place – suppression through medication, breathing techniques, or other methods to create calm and distance to the material usually makes matters worse by cementing the unresolved state.

The result is an even greater fear of everything unexpected and unknown from within – even what otherwise could have been part of good and positive change processes.

As mentioned earlier, society's fear and lack of knowledge about psychedelics itself pose a risk here: if your tentative knowledge is that you can get bothersome "flashbacks" as well as become psychotic and "crazy" for the rest of your life, this will easily color how feelings and other inner states in motion are interpreted. Fear and resistance are then a natural reaction, in the worst case leading to worn-down resistance and "involuntary surrender to madness".

Even when the journey has been well planned and correctly executed, there often remains some residual charge. And if the journey has been a real deep dive into challenging psychological or spiritual issues, it's common to feel a bit fragile and roughed up for a few days. Then, it's also not uncommon to have a headache the next day, and one may generally feel tired and drained. There's no drama in this, and it can resemble the way one feels after other types of major emotional discharges.

First and foremost, it's important to show extra care for oneself in the days after. As part of the preparations for a psychedelic experience, one should also plan for a manageable schedule the following days. Even better is having a few days off, where time to be in nature, bathe or swim, take walks, and listen to music should be central. If you have artistic or creative inclinations, it's good to facilitate free, associative practice of the preferred art form. I also always encourage setting aside some time to listen to the playlist used during the session and to write down the experiences from the journey. It might take a week or two with some keywords or sentences here and there before reaching some kind of conclusion, but this process itself is an important piece in the complete integration of what surfaced during the journey.

Regarding the playlist, it's good to start from the beginning of the list, so that one gently moves into the landscape that was opened during the journey. Most will experience renewed contact, further release, or deeper insights. The music will act as a trigger that once again expands already opened cracks into the psychedelic or mind-manifesting landscape. This way, unresolved remnants of themes, emotions, or bodily resistance can find their way to the surface, rather than us fearing them and trying to push them back. It is important not to suppress or inhibit this, but on the contrary, to help it along. That's also a reason for having an open schedule.

We don't need to dwell in these feelings all the time, but we should set aside a little time each day for a week or two: 5 minutes, 15 minutes, or half an hour. The procedures for this are thoroughly described in Marc Aixalà's book "Psychedelic Integration". Essentially, they involve not trampling the charged material back down to where it came from, but continuing to help it to the surface in manageable portions – based on the individual's life situation and tolerance. A person with generally little substance to cling to will need relatively more time for stabilization and maybe just a few minutes daily or every other day to open up to what rises from within. A person with a generally solid psyche and a safe and stable life can open up faster and to a much greater extent to both good and bad feelings from the muddy bottom of lived life – so that these can rise to the surface and evaporate in the sunlight. In other words: the adult mind can integrate the child's or the lower selves' "truncated experiences" – what has been split off, hidden, and forgotten in the dark corners and closets of our inner being. As with trauma work, it involves creating a safe setting and atmosphere used as a basis for visits into the thematic and emotional remnants after the event.

As stated, the first time after the journey can be "rough" in the sense that you feel both positive changes and painful emotions. It's important not to underestimate this and know that someone preparing for a psychedelic journey has sufficient surplus or support in everyday life to handle such a temporary destabilization. In addition to the themes opened up in the journey, it's also often the case that the experience itself and all its impressions require their own integration. Especially for vulnerable, closed, or rigid personality types, the understanding of reality can be significantly shaken. The same can apply to very young or "naive" people. This must never be underestimated, and is important to consider thoroughly before choosing to embark on a psychedelic journey.

If the "damage is done", and we inadvertently opened up to landscapes one might not really have wished to gain insight into, it's important to take plenty of time to land and frame this in a way that helps the individual find new bearings on their own terms and interpretations. Although one should also help people away from obviously dysfunctional interpretations, it's important not to let one's own philosophy, religion, or other ideological points of view dictate how the other should land what they have experienced.

It's important to emphasize that for the vast majority, this goes very well, all by itself. As a tripsitter or psychedelic guide, however, it's still important to do what one can to facilitate the process and pay extra attention to those who need more follow-up.

## Repeated journeys

Before considering embarking on a new psychedelic journey, all themes, feelings, and impressions from the last experience should have been handled in such a way that they no longer "burn" within us, but have found a new, safe course. Very often, new themes emerge that we feel we need to dive into at some point to continue our own development.

David Nutt writes in his beforementioned book that there seems to be no connection between the various journeys a person takes. This is only apparently or partially true. It is correct that each journey constitutes its own experience, and it's not as predictable as other substances we're accustomed to. However, if one enters this landscape repeatedly, it becomes clear that there are important psychodynamic connections between the journeys. Experientially, a first journey often turns out to be a relatively positive experience, except for those struggling with strong anxiety or major traumas. In such cases it can be very challenging both to enter, go through, and come out of the psychedelic state. The next round, however, often becomes difficult also for those who had a "light" first experience. At least 50% of cases seem to become "darker, totally different," as one client described it. Thus, it's easy to think that there is no connection between the experiences.

Even when we take into account the variables of set and setting, it seems impossible to predict what the next journey will bring. The mindset is naturally impossible to recreate 100% – and when we think about it, that's also kind of the point. We are in a different mental place after a psychedelic journey, which entails several changes: For one, we have experience with letting the psychedelic effects take hold of us and carry us through the journey, as well as often with what it actually means to receive, acknowledge, and "let go" as a physical, conscious event. This typically makes us better able to surrender even more the next time – but not always: A very difficult and poorly integrated journey can also have created fear of surrendering. This must be handled in its own way.

Nevertheless, we have often peeled off some layers off our most obvious neuroses and blockages, and at the very least, we have drilled into them a bit. For many, the path is thus somewhat clearer with regards to later journeys, and the chance that one or more of these will venture into more challenging themes is large. But, as with all such work: It is in encountering these repressed, anxiety-filled themes that we can truly experience liberation. The typical outcome is that if these themes culminate, they become much less of a topic for later journeys – before we possibly start working on the archetypal, universal levels. Then they can come back in a more general guise – and give a sense that we are working with the whole of humanity's consciousness field.

Naturally, there's also a structural similarity between most journeys. That is, they start with certain sensations in the body, then transitioning to more content – whether visual, thematic, emotional, or physical – before the effects gradually subside. Sometimes the experience follows a deviant pattern – for example, something I've observed with the combination of men who have been sexually abused in childhood and later covered up feelings of vulnerability, helplessness, and loneliness with substance abuse. Then, seemingly little or nothing happens until the dose is increased sufficiently for the armor to begin cracking – often accompanied by great discomfort, and even heavy pain. Subsequently, the individual typically breaks down in convulsive crying and, for some reason, often also falls out of the bed they're on and ends up lying or sitting on the floor, regressed to an earlier developmental stage.

Regardless of how a first and second journey unfolds – typically or atypically – aspects that appeared unclear or incomprehensible in the first journeys usually begin to make sense. Perhaps we see them from multiple perspectives, or maybe they reappear over and over until we begin to understand what they're about. Thus, repeated journeys with sufficient time in between for reflection and the best possible integration of impressions from the experiences can become an important part of moving life in a "truer," healthier, and better direction.

# Checklist for psychedelic journeys

| | General check points | If yes: |
|---|---|---|
| 1 | Are you on lithium? (for bipolar dosirder) | Lithium cannot be combined with psychedelics. Bipolar disorder may increase risk of adverse effects after the trip |
| 2 | Are you pregnant, or do you breastfeed? | Postpone your session till after birth and breastfeeding period |
| 3 | Are you on antipsychotics or tranquilizers? | Check online for interactions |
| 4 | Do you have heart problems? | Talk to your physician. In general: If you can enjoy sex and other exciting activities, your system will handle a psychedelic journey |
| 5 | Do you have epilepsy? | Psilocybin or LSD rarely sparks epileptic seizures. Stat low on dosage. Some experience that regular psilocybin microdising increases risk of seizures |

| 5 | Are you on antidepressants? (SSRI/SNRI's) | SSRI/SNRI's may reduce the effect of psychedelics, but the combination is usually not dangerous. Dosage may have to be increased by 30-50% to obtain the psychedelic effect |
|---|---|---|
| 6 | Are you on medication that has to be ingested at certain times, also during the trip? | Let the trip sitter remind you on your medicines during the session |
| 7 | Are you allergic to certain foods or substances? | Talk to the trip sitter |
| 8 | Have you experienced psychotic episodes? | Increased risk of adverse effects. Psychedelics should generally be avoided. If you still want to to try, dosage should be low. Set and setting is *extremely important* |
| 9 | Did anyone in your immedialte family suffer psychotic episodes? | Statistcally increased risk. Set, setting and solid mental preparations are more important than usual |
| 10 | Do you suffer from panic attacks? | Talk to the trip sitter. Good preparations is important |
| 11 | Do you experience anxiety related to health or bodily processes in general? | The condition can make the onset of the trip difficult. Good preparations is important |

| 12 | Are you scared by the unknown, by darkness or the thought of cosmic and spiritual questions? | Talk to the trip sitter. It is important to be prepared for the types of experiences you may have |
|---|---|---|
| 13 | Have you had difficult psychedelic experiences in the past – experiences that have been difficult to integrate? | Seek better these integration of these experiences before a new trip takes place |
| 14 | Do you feel ready for the psychedelic experience? | You should feel ready before taking a psychedelic trip |
| 15 | Do you feel that this is the day to actually go through the psychedelic experience? | You should feel that this is the day for the experience. If "under the weather", postpone the trip |
| 16 | Do you feel safe in the situation? (in the room, with the trip sitter etc.) | The setting should feel comfotable, and you should feel that the trip sitter in question is the right person to guide you through the psychedelic session |
| 17 | Nervousness | Enyone preparing for a psychedlic session is a little nervous. This is completely normal |

## About the author

M.R. Kruken is a philosophically oriented therapist, also specialized in reconstruction and integration of traumatic stress. Since 2001 he has been studying the fascinating field of psychedelics, and has over the last years supported more than 200 individuals on their psychedelic journeys, hence creating a unique base for deep understanding of the processes involved.